Hosanna!

Hosanna!

An Easter Musical for Children

DENIS O'GORMAN & BARRY HART

kevin mayhew

We hope you enjoy *Hosanna!* Further copies are available
from your local music shop or Christian bookshop.

In case of difficulty, please contact the publisher direct by writing to:

The Sales Department
KEVIN MAYHEW LTD
Buxhall
Stowmarket
Suffolk IP14 3BW

Phone 01449 737978
Fax 01449 737834
E-mail info@kevinmayhewltd.com

Please ask for our complete catalogue of outstanding Church Music.

Public performance of this work is allowed only with the permission of the publisher and on condition that the appropriate performance royalty is paid. Please refer to the performance licence form at the back of the book.

First published in Great Britain in 1990 by Fountain Publications.
Reassigned to Kevin Mayhew Ltd. in 2002.

© Copyright 2002 Kevin Mayhew Ltd.

ISBN 1 84003 966 3
ISMN M 57024 121 7
Catalogue No: 1450261

0 1 2 3 4 5 6 7 8 9

The texts and music in this book are protected by copyright and may not be reproduced in any way for sale or private use without the consent of the copyright owner. Please note, the music in this book is *not* covered by a CCL Music Reproduction Licence.

Cover design by Jonathan Stroulger

Printed and bound in Great Britain

Foreword

Hosanna! is a spectacular Easter musical for youngsters written with the Upper Junior/Lower Secondary age ranges in mind. The play, which uses a large cast, is suitable for presentation by schools or church groups. *Hosanna!* begins joyfully with Christ's triumphal entry into Jerusalem and leads us through the events of Holy Week on to a magnificent Pentecost finale when the Holy Spirit is poured out in a colourful scene of dancing wind and fire.

The enclosed free CD not only includes a demo of the songs but also backing tracks for performances where musicians may not be available. *Hosanna!* provides the opportunity for a large-scale musical presentation to celebrate the joyful Good News of Easter.

DENIS O'GORMAN
BARRY HART

Cast

Caiaphas	Mary Magdalene
Annas	Crowd
Jesus	Priests
Peter	Pharisees
John	Soldiers
James	Money Changers
Thomas	Traders
Andrew	Pilgrims
Judas	Apostles
Matthew	Servants
Centurion	Maids
Barabbas	Herod's Entourage
Nicodemus	Angels
Herod	The Fire
Pilate	The Wind

Contents

	Page	*CD Running Order* *Main Track*	*Backing Track*
SCENE 1: JERUSALEM	8		
1. Hosanna!	8	*1*	*16*
2. Hosanna! (Reprise)	14	*2*	*17*
3. Money changed	18	*3*	*18*
4. Hosanna! (Reprise)	21	*4*	*19*
5. Better that only one man dies	24	*5*	*20*
SCENE 2: THE UPPER ROOM	26		
6. Is it me, Lord?	28	*6*	*21*
SCENE 3: GETHSEMANE	32		
7. You must die	34	*7*	*22*
SCENE 4: THE HIGH PRIEST'S HOUSE	37		
8. You're his friend	38	*8*	*23*
SCENE 5: HEROD'S PALACE	40		
9. If you could do a miracle	42	*9*	*24*
10. Hosanna! (Reprise)	46	*10*	*25*
SCENE 6: PILATE'S RESIDENCE	48		
11. Crucify him!	49	*11*	*26*
SCENE 7: CALVARY	50		
12. The sign of love	51	*12*	*27*
SCENE 8: THE UPPER ROOM	54		
13. I've seen the Lord	55	*13*	*28*
14. Hosanna! (Reprise)	60	*14*	*29*
15. Wind and Fire/Hosanna!	63	*15*	*30*

HOSANNA!

Text and Lyrics: Denis O'Gorman
Music: Barry Hart

SCENE 1: JERUSALEM

The stage is empty. The first song is heard in the distance, getting louder and louder until the CROWD appears on stage with JESUS, where they sing it a second time, dancing around him and waving palms.

1. HOSANNA!

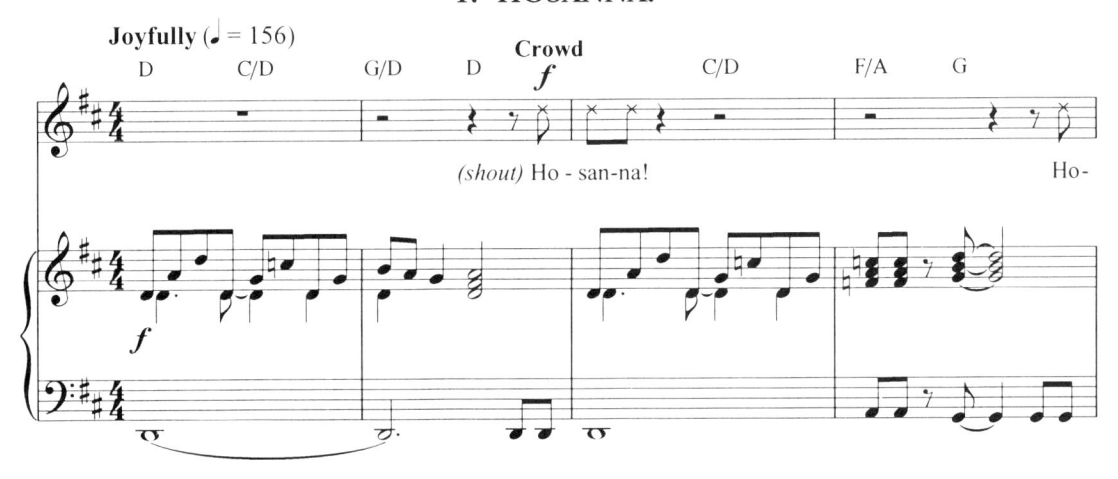

© Copyright 2002 Kevin Mayhew Ltd.
It is illegal to photocopy music.

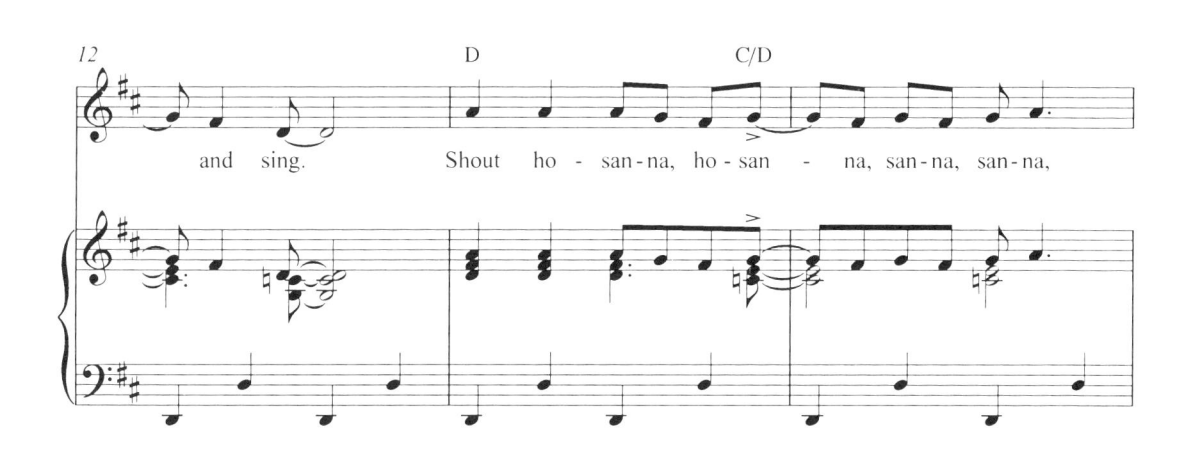

Shout ho-san-na, ho-san - na, san-na, san-na, shout ho-san-na, re-joice and sing. Shout ho-san-na, ho-san - na, san-na, san-na, shout ho-san-na to the King of kings. King of kings. Ho -

-na, Son of Da - vid, hear all your chil-dren sing.

Ho - san - na in the high - est, all pow - er

f ben marcato

to our King! Ho - san - na!

Ho - san - na! Ho -

33
F/C G/B A7sus4
D.S. al Coda
CODA
D C
san - na!
Shout ho - san - na to the
36
D C D C
King of kings,
Shout ho - san - na!
Shout ho - san - na!
39
D C F/A C/G F C/E D
Shout ho - san - na to the King of kings!
ben marcato
42
ff
Ho - san - na!

Enter ANNAS and CAIAPHAS.

Caiaphas	Stop! Stop! Stop this noise! D'you want to start a riot?
1st Person	*(excitedly)* A riot? Yes, that's *just* what we want – a riot!
2nd Person	No more cringing to the Romans!
3rd Person	We want our *freedom!*
4th Person	No more taxes to Caesar!
Annas	*(to JESUS, sarcastically)* So *that's* what you've been teaching them – 'don't pay tax to Caesar.'
Jesus	If you want to know, you'd better ask them.
1st Pharisee	*(to JESUS)* We're asking you! Do they pay or don't they?
Jesus	*(calmly, to the nearest person)* Give me a coin, will you?

The PERSON gives JESUS a coin. JESUS holds it up for everyone to see.

Jesus	*(after a pause)* Whose face is this?
2nd Pharisee	Our noble lord – Tiberius Caesar.

JESUS tosses coin to the 2ND PHARISEE as a CENTURION and TWO SOLDIERS enter from side.

Jesus	Then if it belongs to Caesar, you'd better give it back to Caesar. If it belongs to God, then give it back to God.
Centurion	This is treason! *(to SOLDIERS)* Arrest that man now!
Caiaphas	*(intervening, calmly)* Keep out of this – you'll be destroyed, every one of you!
Barabbas	*(coming forward)* Not without a fight. It'll cost you a dozen legions!
Annas	Barabbas, hold your tongue! D'you want to see the nation ruined?
Barabbas	*(loudly and contemptuously)* I'm not afraid of Caesar. I'd rather die than be his slave!
Centurion	*(to SOLDIERS but looking at BARABBAS – slowly, vindictively)*

Mark that man!

CENTURION and SOLDIERS exit.

Caiaphas *(angrily, to JESUS)* Now see what you've done. Tell this rabble to disperse before you destroy our nation.

JESUS turns and moves away.

Jesus *(turning back once more to PRIESTS and PHARISEES)* If I did, I think these very stones would come alive and sing.

The CROWD begins to sing and follow JESUS off stage.

2. HOSANNA! (Reprise)

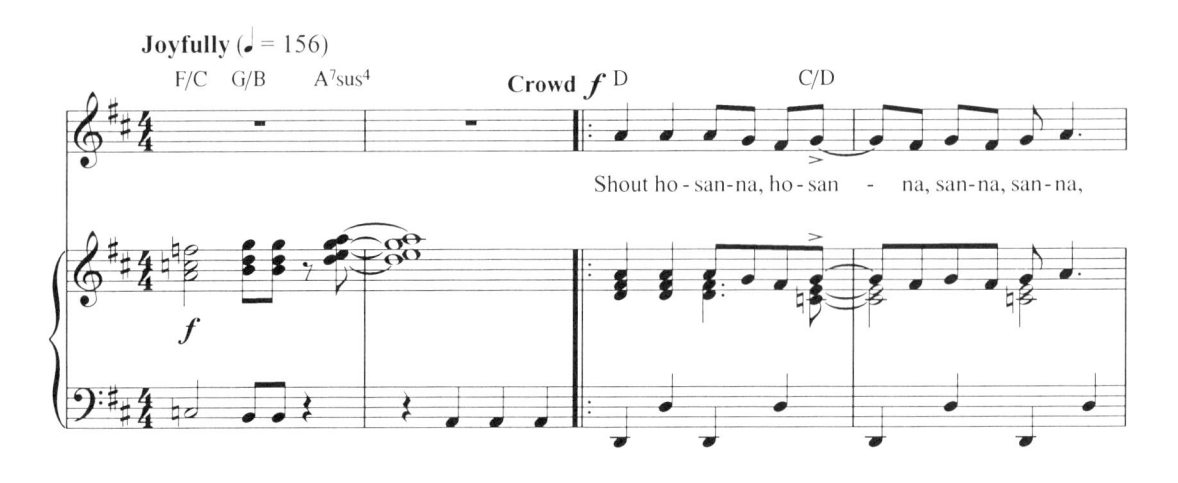

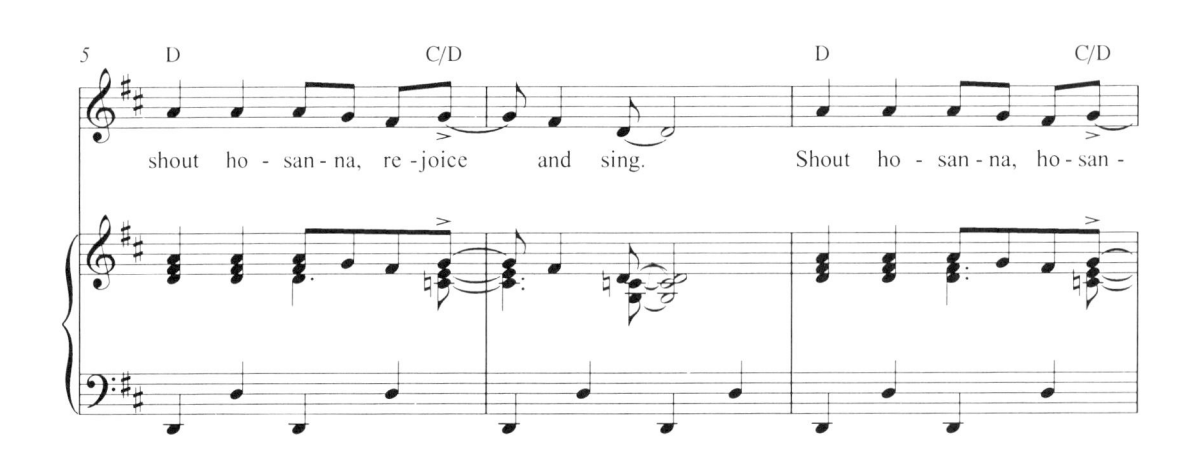

15

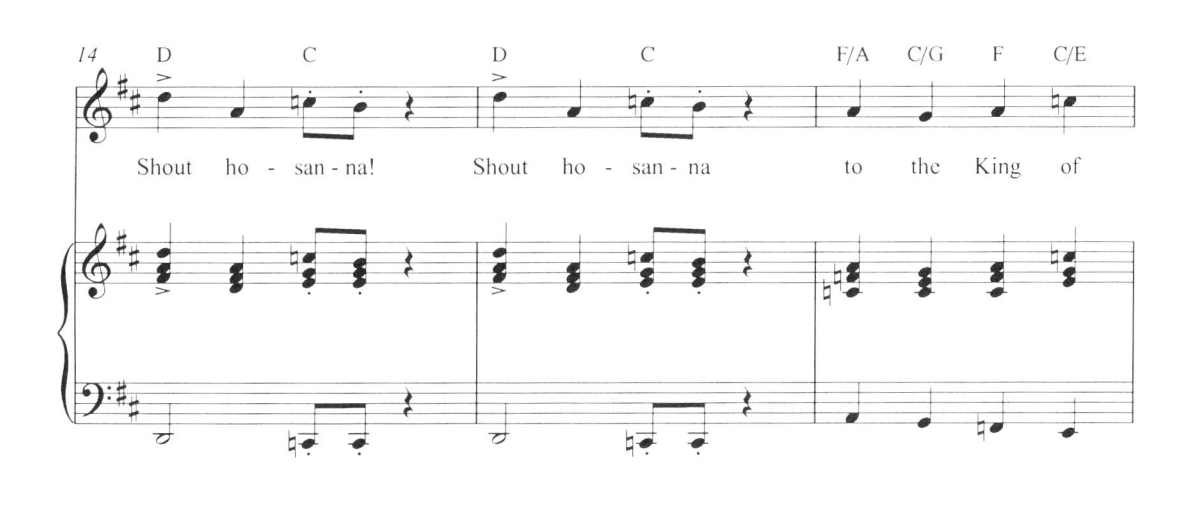

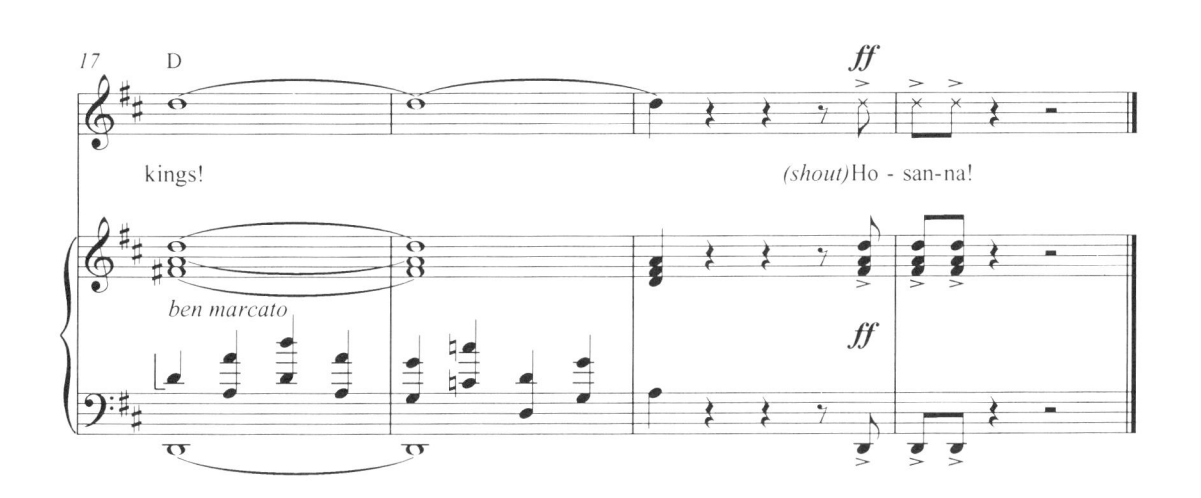

1st Pharisee	*(looking to side of stage)* That man's a danger. What are we going to do?
Caiaphas	*(firmly, without emotion)* He must die. There's no other way to stop him. For their *own* sake, he must die.
1st Pharisee	That won't be easy. The crowds follow him wherever he goes.
Annas	Then we must get him at night, when he's all alone. There must be *someone* who can tell us.
2nd Pharisee	*(eagerly)* I think I know just the person. *(pause, to CAIAPHAS)* But he'll want to be paid.
Caiaphas	*(with authority)* Give him anything he wants – just get him.
2nd Pharisee	*(leaving)* I'll do that, my Lord. Just leave it to me.

2ND PHARISEE leaves. Enter MONEY CHANGERS and TRADERS with large cardboard boxes (stalls), money, lambs, doves etc. They struggle up to CAIPHAS, ANNAS, PRIESTS and PHARISEES.

Trader	*(to CAIAPHAS, urgently)* Excuse me, sir. The pilgrims are coming already. Time's money, you know. Can't miss this lot, can we?
Caiaphas	*(moving out of the way, almost surprised to see them there)* Of course not. Go ahead. *(pause)* And don't forget the Temple treasury.

Traders start to set up their stalls.

Trader	*(cheerfully)* Never do, sir. Ten per cent as usual.
Caiaphas	*(curtly) Fifteen*, this year.
Seller	*(stops setting up stall, astounded)* Oh, come on sir! You don't mean it!
Caiaphas	*(curtly)* Fifteen, or you won't come here again.
Trader	*(despairingly)* We can't charge any more. They wouldn't buy!
Caiaphas	*(unmoved, curtly, moving over to side stage to meet the pilgrims)* They'll have to. They've got no choice.

PILGRIMS enter at side stage, carrying wicker baskets and boxes containing lambs and doves. The PRIESTS go up to look inside and examine the lambs to see if they are without blemish. Some, they allow through, but most have their lambs confiscated and handed to ASSISTANTS and are directed towards the TRADERS and MONEY CHANGERS.

1st Priest *(looking at lambs)* Blemished.

2nd Priest Blemished.

1st Priest Blemished.

2nd Priest Blemished.

The PILGRIMS move up towards the stalls, and there is much commotion as the MONEY CHANGERS and TRADERS sing.

3. MONEY CHANGED

Lively Latin rhythm (♩ = 144)

Money Changers and Traders *mf*

Mo-ney changed! Doves for sale! Lambs for sa-cri-fice! Tell me, won't you buy from me? Change right here! Buy for half the price!

Money Changers and Traders

1. Mo-ney changed! Doves for sale! Lambs for sa-cri-fice!

(2nd and subsequent times only)

2. (Buy for half the price!) Mo-ney changed!

Tell me, won't you buy from me?
Doves for sale! Lambs for sa-cri-fice!

Change right here! Buy for half the price!
Tell me, won't you buy from me? Change right here!

Repeat round until interrupted by Jesus

JESUS enters with his FOLLOWERS. He stares angrily at the scene and interrupts the singing.

Jesus (*shouting*) What have you done to my Father's house?

The commotion dies down and all stare at JESUS.

Jesus (*going up to the stalls and scattering the money, angrily*) Get out, all of you! Get out of here and take your money with you! My Father's house is meant to be a house of prayer and you have made it a den of thieves!

The MONEY CHANGERS scramble to pick up the coins. CAIAPHAS strides over to JESUS.

Caiaphas Your Father's *house*, is it? So now you've brought this rabble back to your Father's *house!*

1st Priest Desecrating the temple on this holy day!

1st Pharisee Who gave you the authority to act like this?

Jesus The works that I do are not my own, but the works of the one who sent me. (*pauses, then firmly*) For the Father and I are *one!*

2nd Priest So now you're equal to God, are you? Is *that* what you're saying?

Jesus If you really knew my Father, you would believe me.

2nd Pharisee Prove it, then. Show us a sign. Then we *may* believe you.

ALL wait for a few moments for his answer.

Jesus (*deliberately*) Destroy this Temple and I will build it up in three days.

Annas It's taken forty years to build this temple. How can you raise it up in three days?

Jesus You asked for a sign. That's the only one I'll give you.

Exit JESUS and his FOLLOWERS and CROWD, singing.

4. HOSANNA! (Reprise)

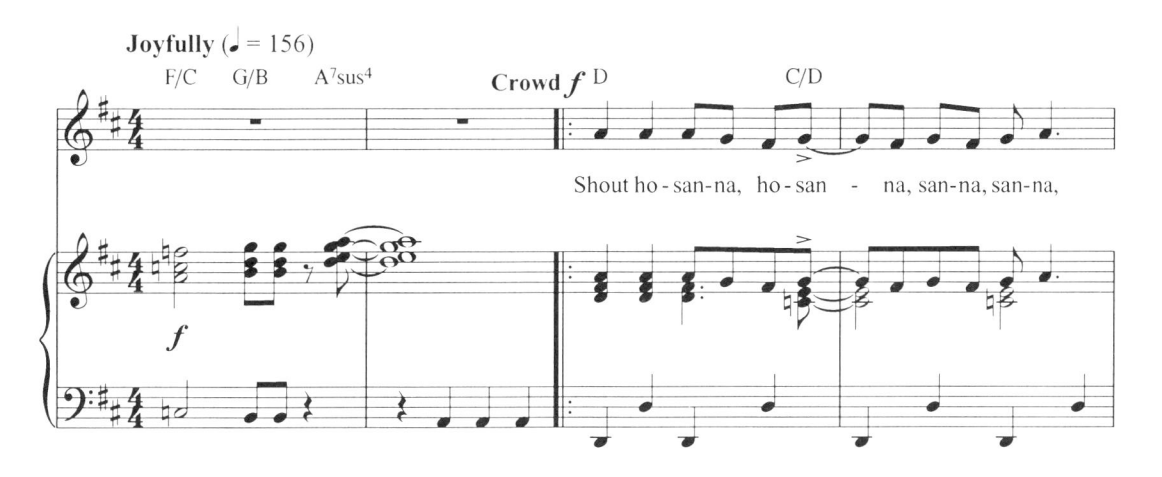

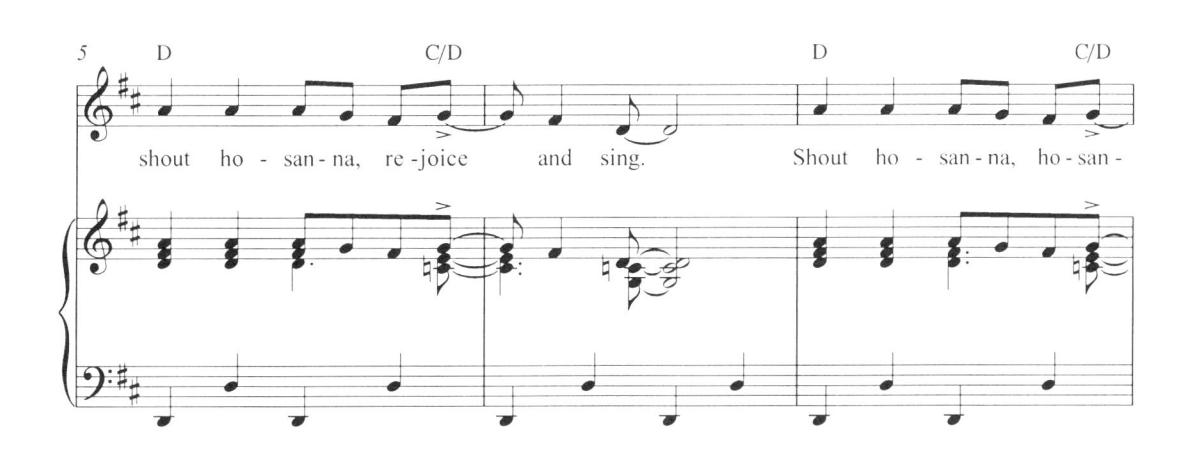

Shout ho-san-na, ho-san - na, san-na, san-na, shout ho-san-na, re-joice and sing. Shout ho-san-na, ho-san - na, san-na, san-na, shout ho-san-na to the King of kings.

11
D C D C
Shout ho - san - na to the King of kings, Shout ho - san - na!
14
D C D C F/A C/G F C/E
Shout ho - san - na! Shout ho - san - na to the King of
17
D
ff
kings! (shout) Ho - san - na!
ben marcato
ff

CAIAPHAS picks up a coin from the floor, and stares at it.

Caiaphas *(calmly and slowly)* Anarchy, chaos, devastation wherever he goes. Gentlemen, we must act now.

Nicodemus *(hesitatingly)* Shouldn't you wait, High Priest. . . *(pause)* just a little longer to see if this *does* come from God?

Caiaphas *(almost kindly)* Nicodemus. You heard him blaspheme. He wants to destroy the Temple. Could *that* come from God?

Nicodemus *(pensively)* I've heard him speak. I saw him cure the sick. Who's to say he's not from God?

Annas And we've all heard him claim to be a king. You know what that means.

3rd Priest The Romans will come and destroy us.

1st Pharisee I agree. We've got to stop him now.

Nicodemus By informing the Romans! Does *that* come from God?

Caiaphas *(impatiently)* Can't you see, Nicodemus? It is better that one man should die than for the whole nation to be lost.

ALL turn to NICODEMUS and sing.

5. BETTER THAT ONLY ONE MAN DIES

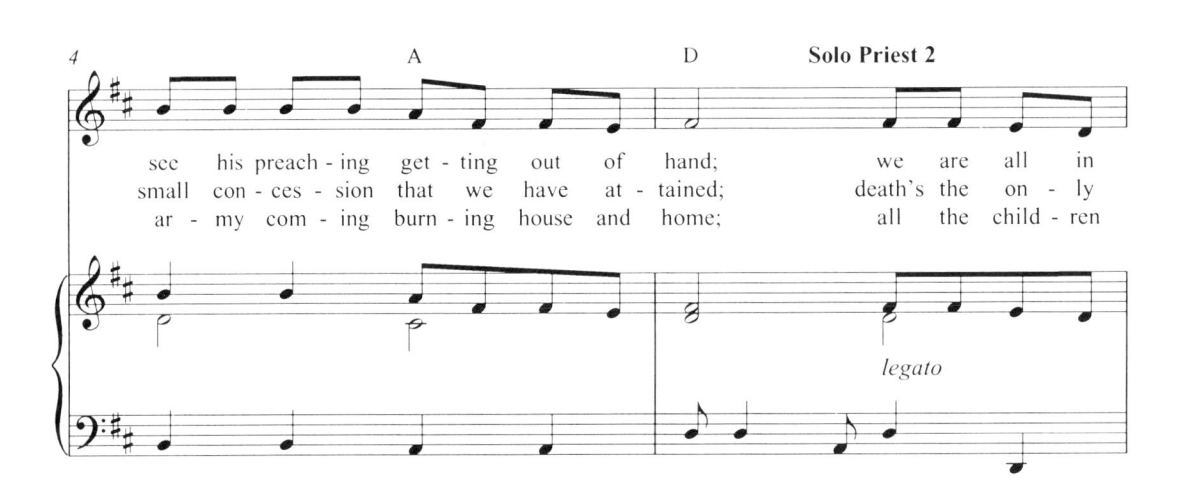

Forceful (♩ = 116)

Solo Priest 1

1. Here is this man walking through the land, I can see his preaching getting out of hand; we are all in danger, so it seems to me, we should save the
render ev-'ry-thing we've gained, ev-'ry small concession that we have attained; death's the only answer, there's no other way, if you love the
see now if this gets to Rome, Caesar's army coming burning house and home; all the children orphaned, strife throughout the land, if we give the

Solo Priest 2

8
Em
1.
F♯7
Solo Priest 1
N.C.
2, 3.
All (except Nicodemus)
mf
na - tion, don't you all a - gree? 2. We'd sur - say. It's
na - tion, let us hear you
rea - son, they will un - der - stand.
11
Em
Bm
cresc. poco a poco
bet-ter that on - ly one man dies, one man dies, one man dies. It's
15
Bm
f
F♯m/A
Gmaj7
Bm/F♯
Solo Priest 1
bet-ter that on - ly one man dies, than all the rest be lost. 3. I fore -
19
2.
Bm/A
Bm/G♯
N.C.
lost, than all the rest be lost.
sfz

After the song, 2ND PHARISEE enters.

2nd Pharisee	*(to ALL, eagerly)* It's all right. He'll do it! Tonight, at ten o'clock.
Caiaphas	*(contemptuously)* At a price, of course.
2nd Pharisee	*(more subdued)* Yes. *(pause)* Thirty pieces of silver.
Caiaphas	No problem. What's his name?
2nd Pharisee	He'd rather not say. Wants to keep it all a secret.
Caiaphas	Fair enough. As long as he does the job, we can forget him.
2nd Pharisee	Then I'll bring him round tonight.
Caiaphas	I shall be waiting. *(pause, to ALL)* Now get some sleep, gentlemen. We shall meet again at twelve. I think we're in for a long night.

Exit CAIAPHAS, followed by the others.

SCENE 2: THE UPPER ROOM

JESUS and APOSTLES gather round a table with bread and wine, herbs, lamb.

Jesus	*(sharing food with APOSTLES)* Ever since we first met, I have longed to share this meal with you.

JUDAS slips away. JESUS moves among the APOSTLES with a loaf which he breaks and gives a piece to each one. All the APOSTLES begin to eat the bread.

Jesus	*(pause)* This is not *bread* that I give to you!

The APOSTLES stop eating and stare at JESUS, puzzled.

Jesus	*(gently, pensively)* This is my *body* that I give to you.

The APOSTLES all eat the bread, still puzzled but more reverently. JESUS takes the cup of wine and hands it to JOHN.

Jesus	*(to JOHN, gently)* This is not *wine* that I give to you. *(pause)* This is my *blood*.

The APOSTLES all pass round the cup. JESUS walks behind them, stops behind PETER and ANDREW and puts his arms round them.

Jesus *(to PETER and ANDREW, kindly)* Whenever you do this together, *(pause)* remember me.

The APOSTLES continue to share the bread and cup reverently. JESUS walks a short distance away and then turns again.

Jesus *(more loudly)* And yet *one* of you betrays me!

The APOSTLES stop eating and look at one another.

Peter *(to JESUS)* I'd never betray you, even if the others do.

Jesus turns away from PETER.

Jesus *(quite abruptly)* Tonight, you will deny me three times *(turns back to PETER, more gently)* but I know you won't betray me.

John Then who *will*, Lord? Tell us now!

Jesus A traitor, who's already shared this meal with me tonight.

James That could be any *one* of us! Say it isn't me, Lord!

Over the song introduction, the APOSTLES protest – 'say it isn't me', 'I'd never betray you.' 'It can't be me.' 'I wouldn't betray you.' Then their protests turn into the song.

6. IS IT ME, LORD?

17 **Group 2** **Groups 1 & 2**

me, Lord. It's not me, Lord. Give us his name but say it isn't

21

me. It can't be Si-mon that you mean,

25 **Group 2**

Pe-ter, James or John. Tell us who's the trai-tor, point him

29 **Group 1**

out be-fore he's gone. If you tell us who he is we'll

33
C Bdim Am G F C
Groups 1 & 2 f
stop him right a - way –
please tell us now, Lord,
f
37
Dm7 G G/A Gmaj7/A
Group 1 mf
quick, we can't de - lay.
Is it
mf
3
40
D F♯m
Group 2
Group 1
Group 2
me, Lord? Is it me, Lord? It can't be, Lord. It can't be, Lord.
44
Em A D Em/A Gmaj7/A
Groups 1 & 2
Group 1
Oh, can't you see, oh, can't you see?
Hear my

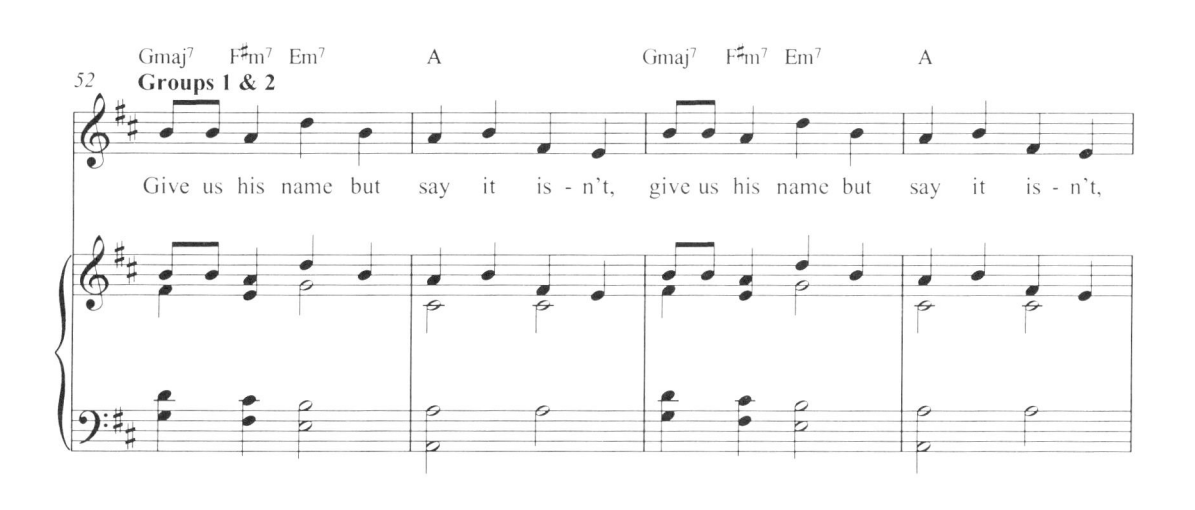

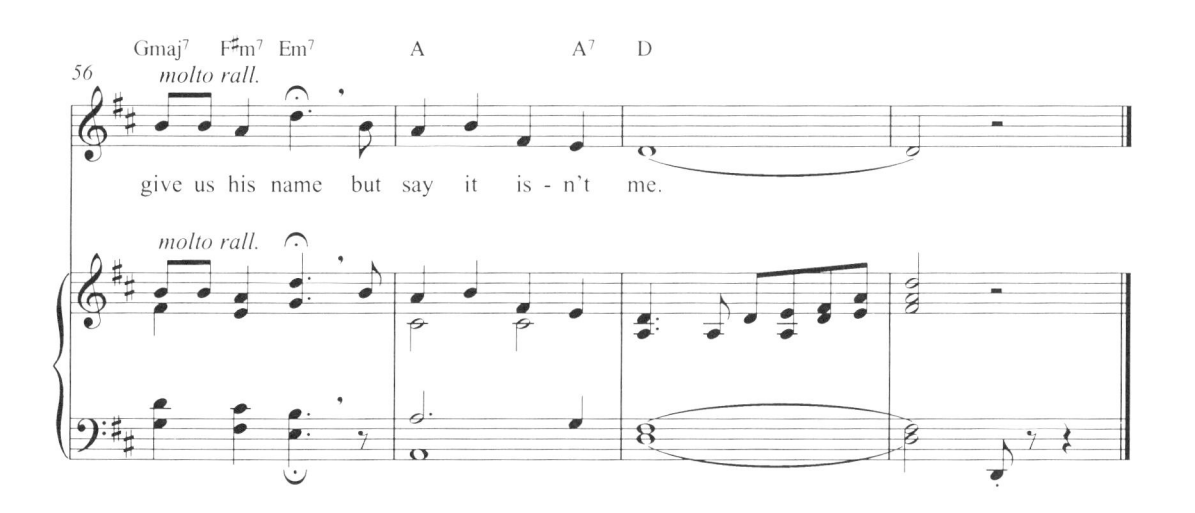

plea, Lord. Hear my plea, Lord. It's not me, Lord. It's not me, Lord.

Give us his name but say it isn't, give us his name but say it isn't,

give us his name but say it isn't me.

| **Jesus** | It doesn't matter now. Come with me to the Garden and pray for the strength to carry on. |

SCENE 3: GETHSEMANE

JESUS goes to the centre/front of the stage and kneels. The APOSTLES kneel behind him in a semicircle. As they pray silently for a while, the accompaniment to the previous song could be played slowly in the background. One by one, the APOSTLES grow tired and fall asleep.

| **Jesus** | *(looking up towards heaven)* Father, if there's a way out of this, show me; if not – give me courage. |

JESUS prays silently for a while; then stands up and turns to the sleeping APOSTLES. He walks behind them, quietly, watching them sleep. He gently goes across and stands behind PETER who is fast asleep.

| **Jesus** | *(to PETER)* Peter, couldn't you watch with me for an hour? *(pause, with compassion, kindly as if to a sleeping child)* You mean well *(pause)* but you never seem to get things right. |

JESUS looks towards side stage and then back at the sleeping APOSTLES.

| **Jesus** | Sleep on, my friends, and take your rest, for now those evil men are on their way. |

A few moments later, JUDAS, PRIESTS and SOLDIERS rush in. JUDAS goes up to JESUS to embrace him, but JESUS sidesteps him and brushes him off.

| **Jesus** | *(angrily, to JUDAS)* Judas! Don't betray me with a kiss! |

The impetus of the sidestep propels JUDAS towards the APOSTLES, who suddenly wake up as he staggers among them.

| **Peter** | *(to JUDAS, suddenly realising what is happening)* Judas! |

| **Andrew** | You traitor! |

JUDAS tries to run away.

| **James** | Get him! |

The SOLDIERS grab hold of JESUS. The APOSTLES grab their swords. Some follow JUDAS, others attack the SOLDIERS.

| **Jesus** | *(amidst the turmoil)* Put away your swords! |

The fighting continues but the APOSTLES are beaten back.

Jesus *(louder)* Put away your swords!

The APOSTLES run away.

Caiaphas *(stepping forward, to JESUS, angrily)* Now will you destroy the Temple?

Annas *(with sarcasm and fury)* King of the Jews!

Caiaphas *(with venom, to JESUS)* You're condemned!
(to SOLDIERS) Take him to Pilate!

As they begin to take JESUS away, NICODEMUS intervenes.

Nicodemus Wait!

All stop and look at NICODEMUS, startled and puzzled.

Nicodemus *(calmly, slowly and with dignity)* Is it right to condemn a man without a trial?

Caiaphas *(sharply)* You heard what he said! *(pause, then sarcastically to NICODEMUS)* Or have you become one of his disciples?

Nicodemus *(slowly, firmly, calmly)* Every man is entitled to defend himself in a court.

Caiaphas There's no time for that. He's blasphemed. What more evidence do we need?

7. YOU MUST DIE

guitar plays melody
All (except Nicodemus)
Em B Em
You must die, die, die, don't you see You must
D G Am D7
die, die, die, that's for sure. You must die for the sake of
G C Am Bm Am/F♯ B
ev - 'ry - one, for you claim that you're God's e - ter - nal Son,
Em C/E G/D A/C♯ 1. Em/B B7 Em
this must be done for the sake of the law – you must die, die, die, that's for sure.

2.

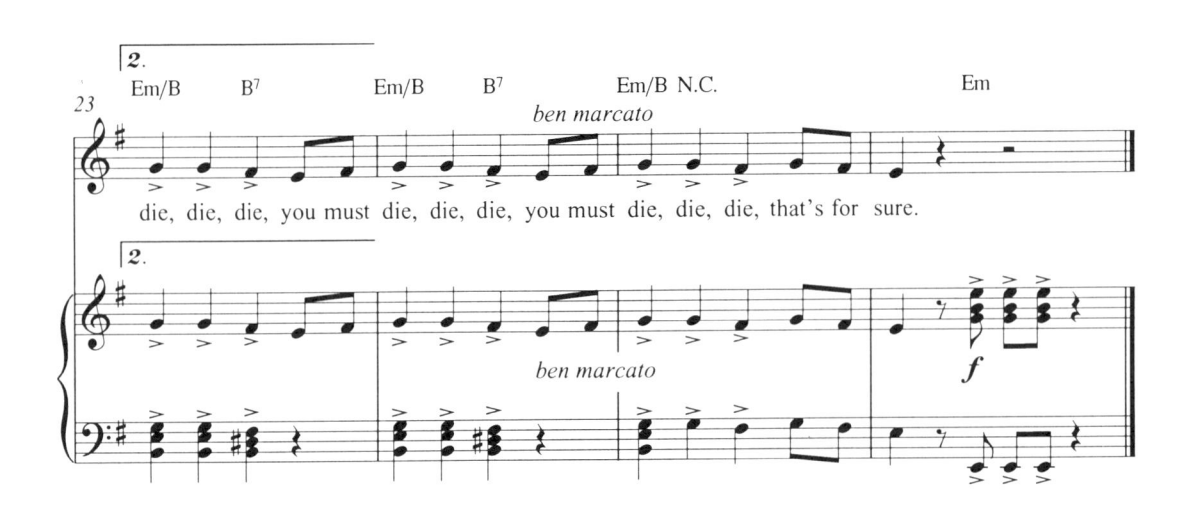

ben marcato

die, die, die, you must die, die, die, you must die, die, die, that's for sure.

At the end of the song, they hustle JESUS off stage. NICODEMUS leaves from the opposite side.

Enter SERVANTS and MAIDS excitedly as if in chase. They 'babble' excitedly:

SCENE 4: THE HIGH PRIEST'S HOUSE

Servants / Maids	Did you see him? There's going to be a riot over this. Pilate won't like this. He can't stand the High Priest. They want to have him crucified. Pilate won't let it happen.

Enter PETER from opposite side of stage.

Peter	*(to MAIDS and SERVANTS)* What's going on here? Sounds to me as if there's been some trouble.
1st Maid	*(to PETER)* It's that man, Jesus. They've taken him to Pilate.
2nd Maid	He's going to be crucified.
Peter	*(disturbed and shocked)* Why? What has he done?
Servant	*(mockingly)* Nearly caused a riot – that's all!
1st Maid	What are you worried about, anyway? *(pause, mockingly)* You're not one of his friends, are you?
Peter	No, I was just passing by.
2nd Maid	*(with glee and sudden realisation)* Yes, you are! I saw you at Cana.
Peter	*(frightened and disturbed)* It wasn't me. I've never met him.
1st Maid	*(pushing PETER)* It must have been. You're a Galilean! I can tell by your accent!
Peter	Leave me alone, will you! *(shouting)* I *swear* I don't know the man!

All gather round and sing, making sport of PETER, who tries to get away but is cornered every time.

8. YOU'RE HIS FRIEND

Accusingly - vigorous tempo ($\quarter = 146$)

All *f*

You're his friend, don't deny it. You're his friend, don't deny it. You're his friend, don't deny it. You're his friend!

Last time to Coda

Soloists *mf*

1. You were in the garden, standing by his side,
2. Now we know for certain, now we know for sure,
3. Now we've really got you, fighting to survive,

when you heard the soldiers,
we are not mistaken,
claiming you don't know him,

16

then you tried to hide.	Then we near-ly
we've seen you be-fore.	You can-not de-
just to stay a-live.	There's no one to

19

caught you	but you ran too fast,
ceive us,	we see through your lies,
help you,	no-where you can go,

22

now we've got you cor-nered,	in our hands at
you're a Ga-li-le-an,	that you can't dis-
can't you see it's o-ver,	we al-rea-dy

25 — Asus⁴ — A — guitar plays melody — CODA — Dm

last.	You're his friend!
guise.	
know.	

sfz

At the end of the song, PETER manages to escape and the others chase him off stage.

SCENE 5: HEROD'S PALACE

Enter HEROD'S SOLDIERS bearing large colourful shields and banners. They form a line across the back of the stage and place their shields in front of them to form a background of pageant and power. Enter SERVANTS with bowls of fruit, wine etc. They stand in front of, and in between the SOLDIERS to add a touch of opulence to the background.

Enter HEROD with 'adoring' LADY COMPANIONS. He is talking to them 'sotto voce'. He could be saying anything but the suggestions below could be used:

Herod (*sotto voce*) . . . and then I said, 'You may be a Roman Governor, but I'm a king.' *(peals of laughter)* . . . you should have seen his face. I thought he was going to drop dead. *(peals of laughter)* . . . and then I said, 'Never mind, you can come and stay here for a few days, when you get fed up with your tiny barracks!' *(peals of laughter)*

HEROD, very pleased that he is making such an 'impression' on the ladies, offers them food and wine. HEROD bites an apple and turns to side stage.

Herod All right, then. Show him in.

Enter ANNAS, CAIAPHAS and PRIESTS with JESUS.

Herod	So *this* is the man we've heard so much about. *(goes up to JESUS)* I've been waiting so long to see you.
1st Priest	He claims he's a *king*. Pilate wants you to sentence him to death.
Herod	Surely Pilate can do that for himself! Why send him to *me?*
2nd Priest	Because he's a Galilean. He's your responsibility.
Herod	*(with feigned shock and amusement)* Is that what he said? *(pause, with exaggerated delight)* I'm overwhelmed by this sudden recognition of my authority. *(pause, to LADIES)* Though I imagine that cunning serpent has other motives.
Annas	*(emphatically)* This man has been stirring up the crowds to make him *king* instead of *you!*
Herod	*(with mock geniality and friendliness)* Oh, Annas. All these years I've misjudged you. I didn't realise how loyal you were.
Caiaphas	He also claims to be the Son of God!
Herod	*(with a look of disappointment)* Now don't spoil it, Caiaphas. *(like a spoilt child)* You know I'm not interested in religion.
Caiaphas	It affects you just the same. If people think he's God, they'll make him king!
Herod	*(with mock surprise and concern)* I never thought of that. *(pause, with glee)* Let's give him a chance to prove it. *(to JESUS)* One little miracle will do.

HEROD bursts into song, showing off for all he is worth and using mocking actions which fit the words – presenting JESUS with water, precious stones etc. The feeling of ridicule is heightened by HEROD'S ENTOURAGE joining in, as indicated, backing-group style.

9. IF YOU COULD DO A MIRACLE

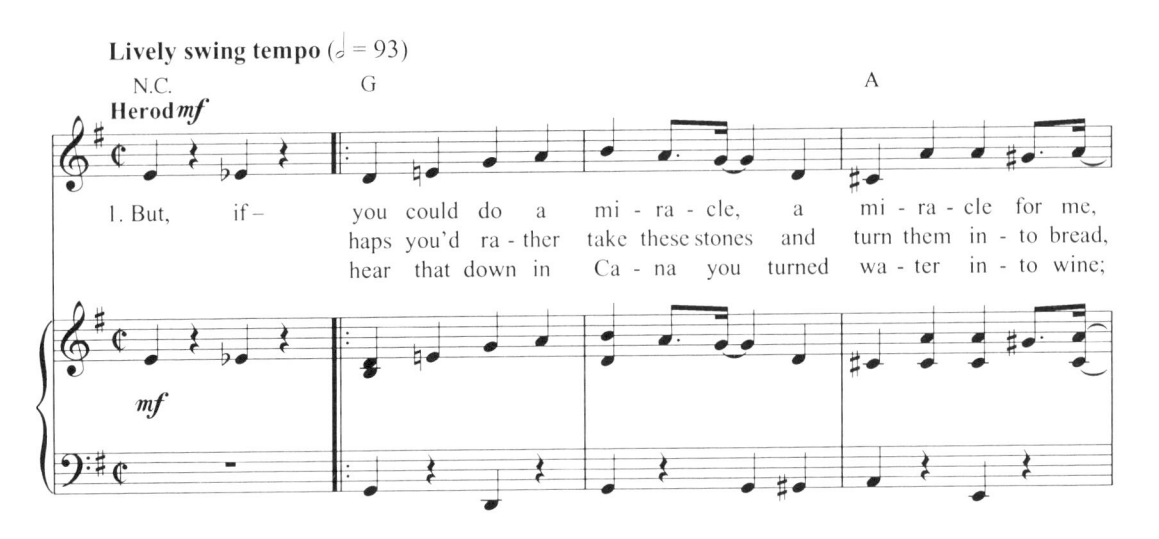

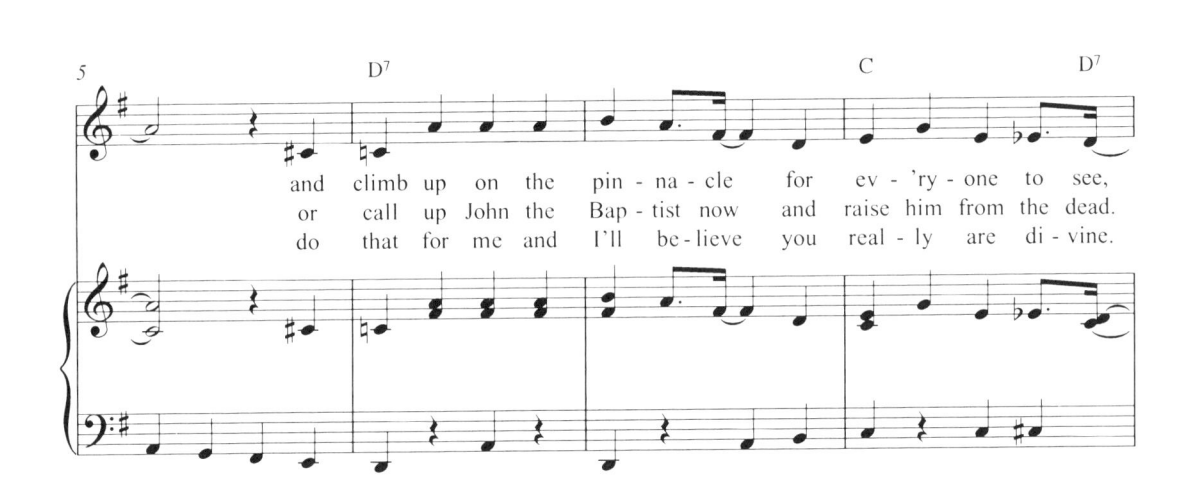

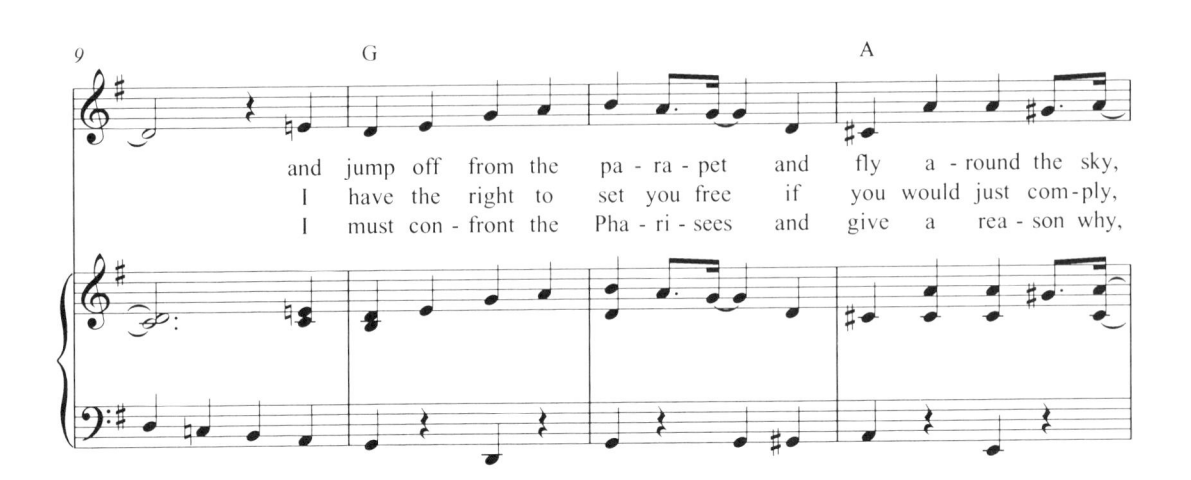

Lively swing tempo ($\n = 93$)

Herod *mf*

1. But, if – you could do a mi - ra - cle, a mi - ra - cle for me,
   and climb up on the pin - na - cle for ev - 'ry - one to see,
   and jump off from the pa - ra - pet and fly a - round the sky,

   haps you'd ra - ther take these stones and turn them in - to bread,
   or call up John the Bap - tist now and raise him from the dead.
   I have the right to set you free if you would just com - ply,

   hear that down in Ca - na you turned wa - ter in - to wine;
   do that for me and I'll be - lieve you real - ly are di - vine.
   I must con - front the Pha - ri - sees and give a rea - son why,

42

I'll see to it, you won't die. You won't die, you won't die. I'll see that you won't (He'll) die; if you could do a miracle I'll see that you won't (he'll) die.

2. Per-
3. I

Lyrics:

you could do a mi-ra-cle, if you could do a mi-ra-cle, if you could do a mi-ra-cle, (he'll) I'll see that you won't die!

HEROD finishes with a flourish. SERVANTS and LADIES applaud.

Caiaphas There you are. He doesn't even speak.

Annas He can't work miracles, either. Never has!

Herod *(going up to JESUS, with contempt)* So you're not a king or God, after all. How very disappointing. Still, we mustn't disappoint your followers. I think we should have a little coronation.

HEROD takes off his purple cloak and places it on JESUS.

Herod *(to all, with a great flourish)* The *King* of the *World! (all applaud and laugh)* Take him back to Pilate. We shall form a royal escort to the palace gates.

PRIESTS and entourage grab hold of JESUS and lead him away. HEROD, LADIES and SERVANTS follow, singing in mockery.

10. HOSANNA! (Reprise)

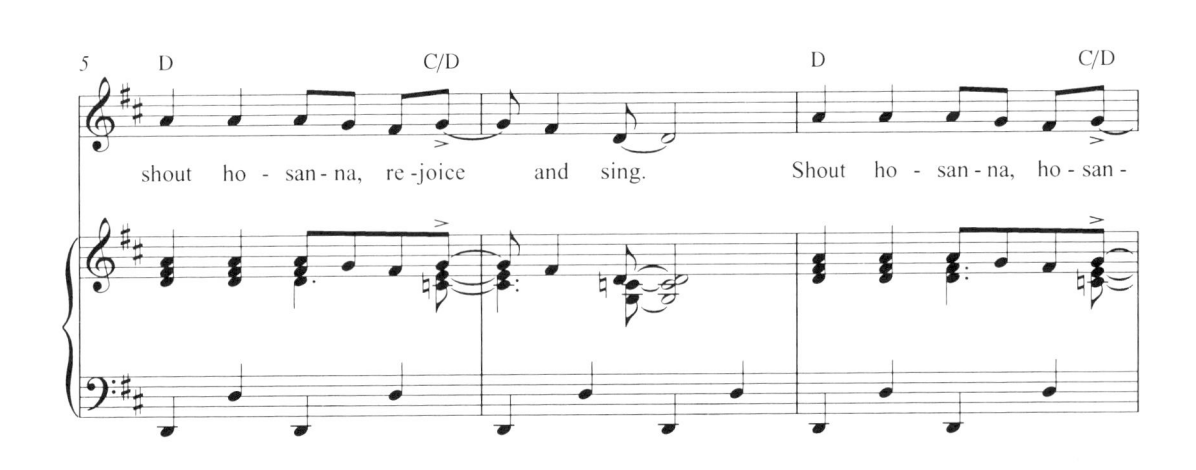

Mockingly (♩ = 156)

All *f*

Shout ho-san-na, ho-san - na, san-na, san-na, shout ho-san-na, re-joice and sing. Shout ho-san-na, ho-san - na, san-na, san-na, shout ho-san-na to the King of kings.

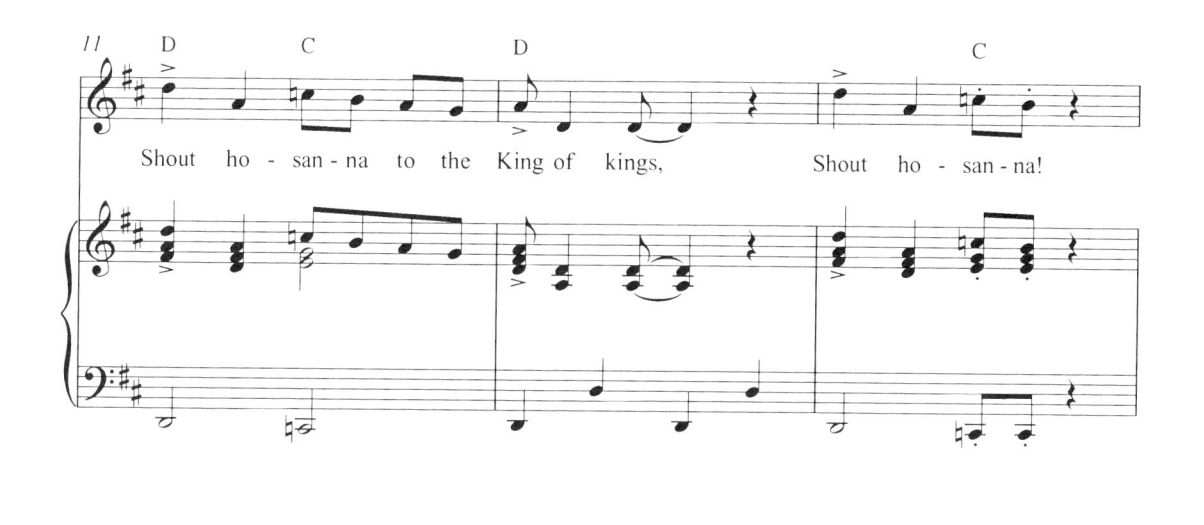

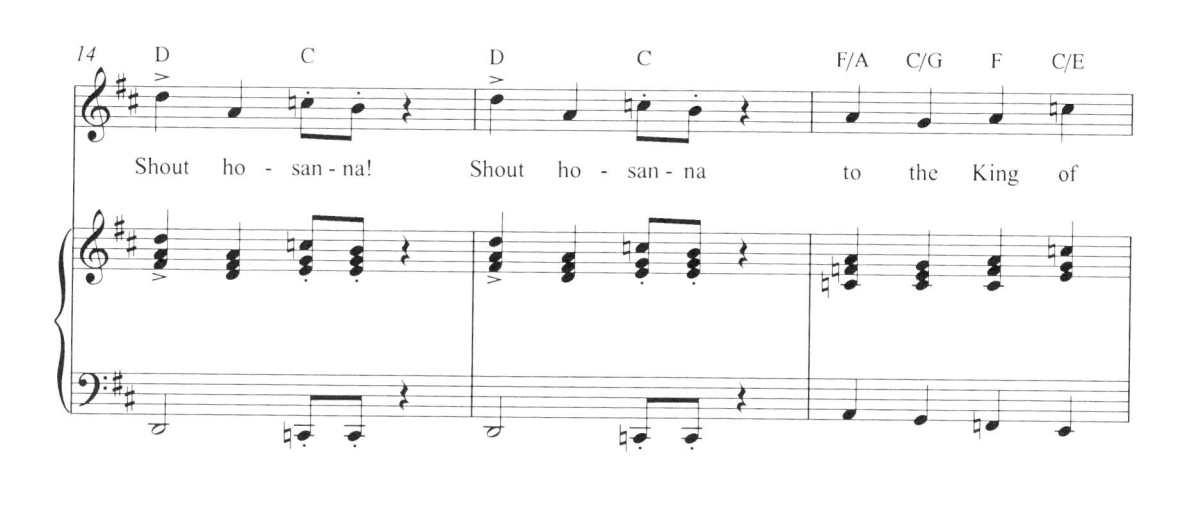

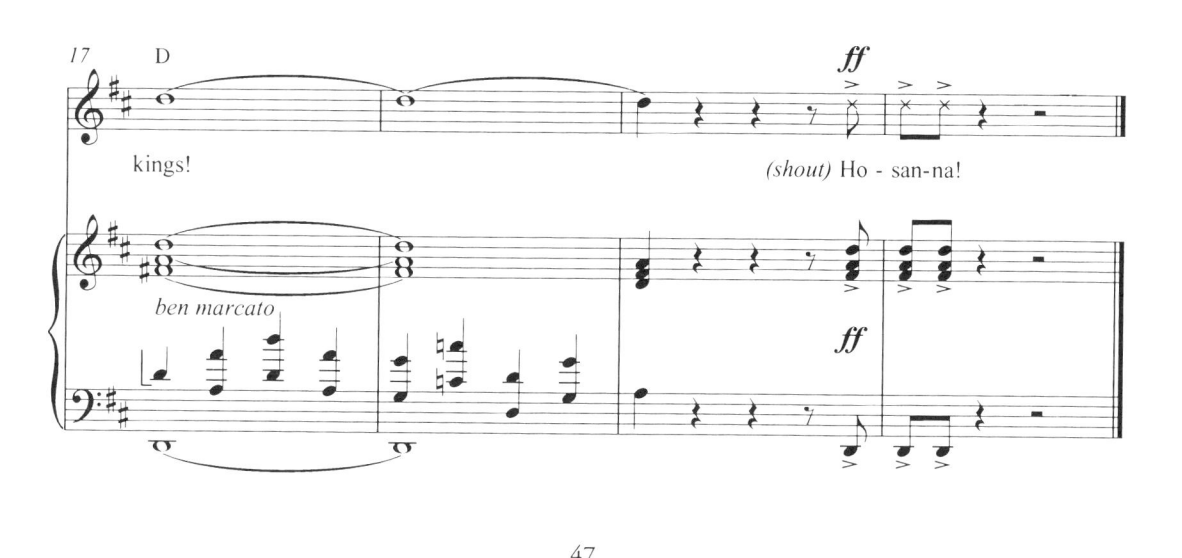

Shout ho-san-na to the King of kings, Shout ho-san-na!

Shout ho-san-na! Shout ho-san-na to the King of

kings! *(shout)* Ho-san-na!

ben marcato

47

SCENE 6: PILATE'S RESIDENCE

Enter PRIESTS and CROWD with JESUS. Enter PILATE with a SOLDIER on each side.

Pilate	So you're back already? That didn't take long. *(picks up folds of the purple cloak)* I see Herod thinks you're just a joke. *(pause)* So do I. *(to SOLDIER, abruptly)* Have him flogged and then release him.

PILATE begins to move off.

Caiaphas	Do that, and you're no friend of Caesar.

PILATE turns back.

Pilate	Then go and crucify him yourselves!
Annas	Only you can do that!
Pilate	*(to JESUS, disturbed)* You've heard their accusations. Why don't you answer them?
Jesus	My kingdom is not of this world.
1st Priest	We have no king but Caesar!
2nd Priest	You can't release him! He has defied Rome!
Pilate	So has Barabbas! But Rome decrees that I must set one of them free!
Annas	No, Pilate. The *choice* is *ours,* and we want Barabbas.
Pilate	Then what shall I do with this Jesus?
Caiaphas	(shouting) Crucify him!
Annas	Don't release him!
1st Priest	Caesar's threatened!
2nd Priest	Don't defy him!
3rd Priest	Herod's angry!
4th Priest	Pacify him!
Annas	Free Barabbas!
Caiaphas	Crucify him!

11. CRUCIFY HIM!

Menacingly (♩ = 120)

Lyrics:

Cru-ci-fy him! Don't re-lease him! Cae-sar's threat-ened! Don't de-fy him! Free Ba-rab-bas! Don't de-ny him! He-rod's an-gry! Pa-ci-fy him! Cru-ci-fy him! Cru-ci-fy him! Cru-ci-fy him! Cru-ci-fy him! Cru-ci-fy him! Cru-ci-fy him!

guitar plays melody

Pilate	*(angrily)* All right. Let him be crucified. But don't blame me! I wash my hands of this whole affair.

The two SOLDIERS grab JESUS and drag him off. The CROWDS disperse with 'babble'.

SCENE 7: CALVARY

SOLDIERS enter and erect a large cross front centre stage. The CROWD gathers round, looking at the cross, facing the audience. SOLDIERS play dice at the foot of the cross.

Caiaphas	*(looking up at the cross)* If you could rebuild the Temple in three days, why don't you save yourself?
1st Soldier	*(throwing dice)* Ten!
Annas	He saved others but he can't save himself!
2nd Soldier	*(throwing dice)* Six!
1st Priest	If you are the Son of God, come down from the cross and we'll believe you.
2nd Soldier	*(throwing dice)* Three!
2nd Priest	If you're really the King of Israel, come down from the cross.
1st Person	Listen. He's calling on Elijah. Let's see if anything happens.
Loud voice	*(off stage)* Forgive them, Father. Into your hands I commend my spirit.
3rd Soldier	Truly, this was the Son of God.

Thunder and rain are heard. The stage is darkened. The CROWDS leave briskly with 'babble'.

Voices in crowd	Let's get away from this place. Look at those clouds. Give me a hand. I can't see where I'm going. We shouldn't have come here. Listen to that thunder.

Choir, off-stage or ANGELS (with simple white robes) on stage gathering round the cross, sing.

12. THE SIGN OF LOVE

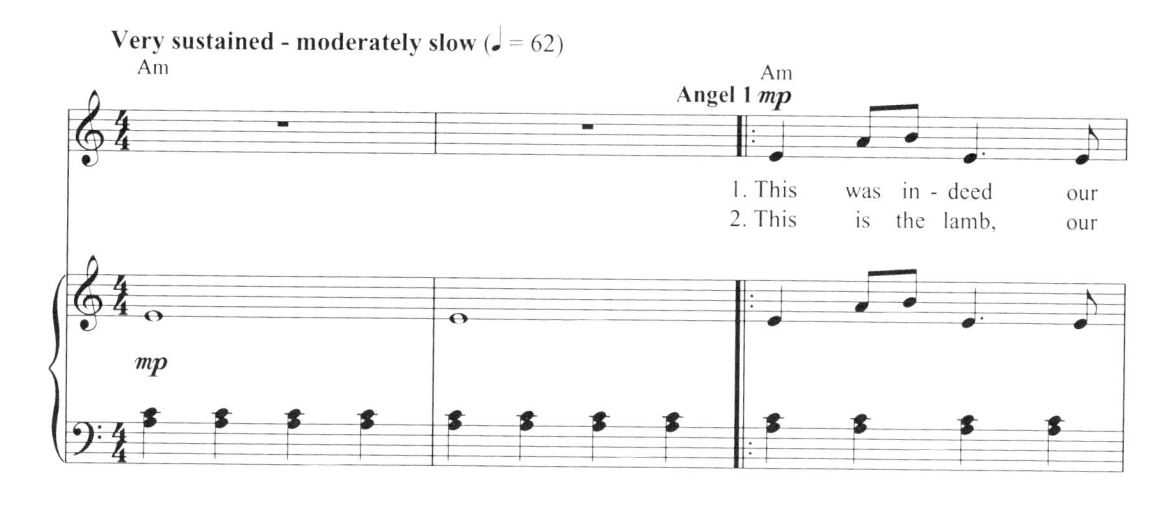

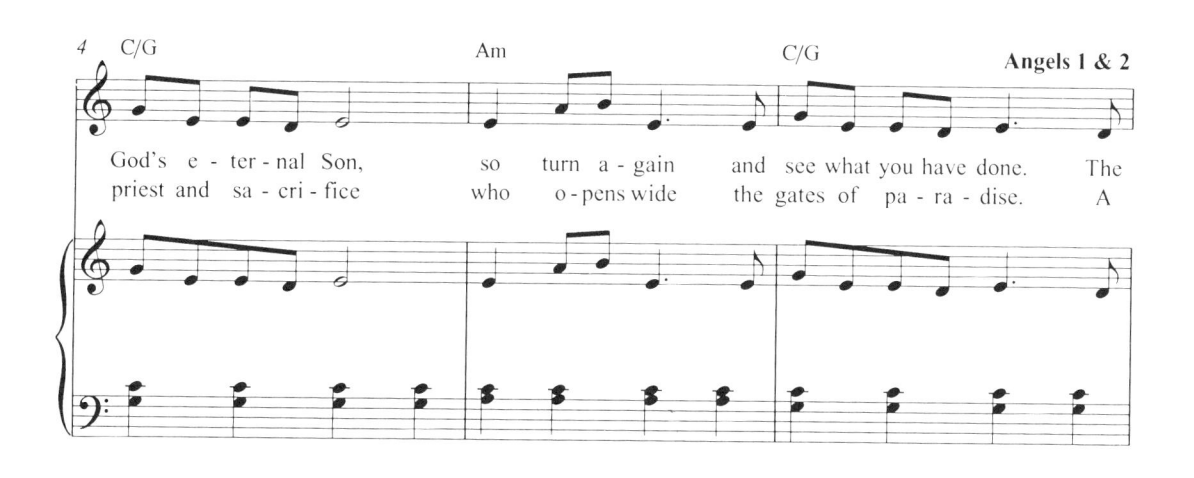

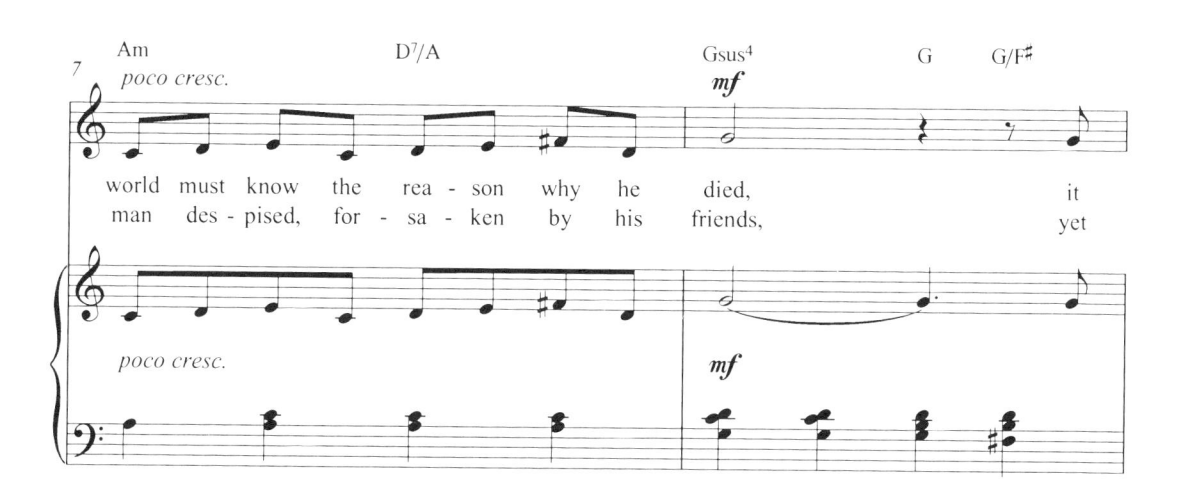

Very sustained - moderately slow ($\quarternote = 62$)

Angel 1 mp

1. This was in-deed our God's e-ter-nal Son, so turn a-gain and see what you have done. The world must know the rea-son why he died, it
2. This is the lamb, our priest and sa-cri-fice who o-pens wide the gates of pa-ra-dise. A man des-pised, for-sa-ken by his friends, yet

Angels 1 & 2

poco cresc.

was for sins that he was cru-ci-fied.
of-fers still a love that ne-ver ends. So

Angels look a-gain, so look a-gain, and you will see the sign,

look and you will see the sign of love. So look a-gain, so look a-gain, and

you will see the sign, look and you will see the sign of love.

love. *[ANGELS leave. SOLDIERS come on and remove the cross]*

SCENE 8: THE UPPER ROOM

Enter THOMAS, followed by APOSTLES. He stands by the door and urges them on.

Thomas Quick. Hurry. Get some sacks. Anything at all.

The APOSTLES go to the other side of the stage, and bring sacks which they pile against the door. THOMAS goes to the other side of the stage.

Thomas (*in an authoritative tone*) Now, if they come, there's some steps down here, leading to the lane outside. After that, it's every man for himself.

Peter (*stunned, slowly, in a daze*) We let them *take* him!

Thomas (*curtly*) Forget it, Peter. Go back to your fishing.

John (*to THOMAS, hurt by his remark*) Would you forget that quickly, Thomas?

Thomas (*quite embittered*) He let us down, you know. You realise that, don't you? (*pause*) All those promises about his kingdom.

Andrew (*upset*) You don't seem to care at all, Thomas.

Thomas (*turning on them – very upset*) Of course I care! Just as much as the rest of you. But now I want to forget!

A banging is heard on the door. All go quiet.

Thomas (*to others, quietly*) Swords. (*pause*) Quiet.

They all get out their swords and move stealthily towards the door. The banging is heard again.

Mary Magdalene (*from outside*) Open up. It's only me – Mary Magdalene!

James (*pointing to some sacks*) Quick, take them out of the way!

Mary Magdalene (*from outside*) Hurry up. I've got something to tell you.

Thomas All right, Mary. We're nearly there.

Once the sacks have been removed, they pretend to open the door and MARY MAGDALENE comes in.

Peter (*concerned and surprised*) Mary, what are you doing here?

Mary Magdalene (*full of joy and excitement*) I've seen him!

Thomas What do you mean?

Mary Magdalene (*excitedly*) I've seen the Lord!

As the introduction to the song is played, MARY MAGDALENE dances with joy all around the room. In her excitement she goes from one APOSTLE to the other as she sings.

13. I'VE SEEN THE LORD

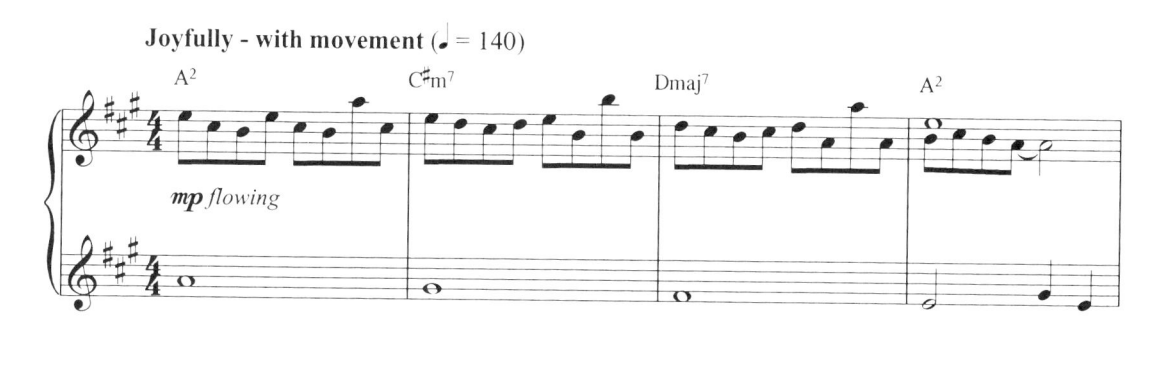

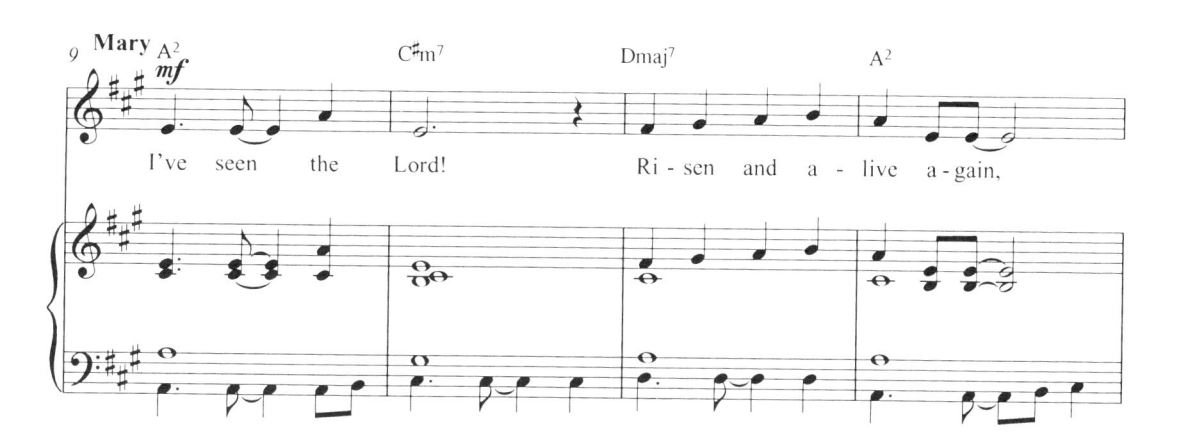

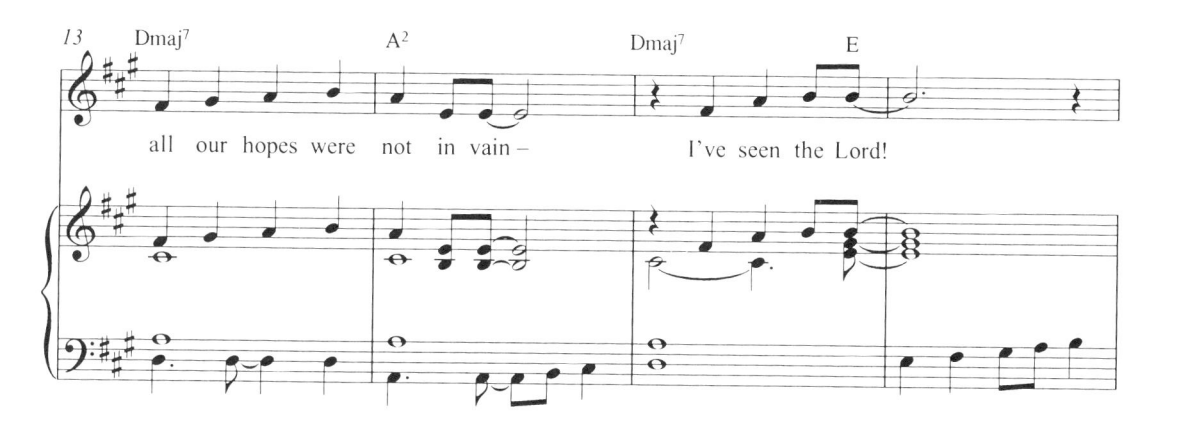

Joyfully - with movement ($\quarternote$ = 140)

mp flowing

mf

Mary

mf

I've seen the Lord! Ri-sen and a-live a-gain,

all our hopes were not in vain – I've seen the Lord!

17
F♯m C♯m Dmaj7 A Esus4 E7
There he stood in front of me, I won - dered who this man could be, then
21
A2 E/G♯ F♯m D/E A2
I looked up and I could see it real - ly was the Lord!
25
C♯m F♯m C♯m F♯m
mp
Cast all your fears a-way, new hope has dawned to-day.
29
D A Bm D/E
mf
mp
Sing with me! Dance with me! For I've come to tell you all that

I've seen the Lord! By the tomb at break of day, where the stone was rolled a-way – I've seen the Lord! 'Ma-ry, weep no more,' he said, 'You see I've ri-sen from the dead, I want you to go on a-head and say you've seen the Lord!'

58

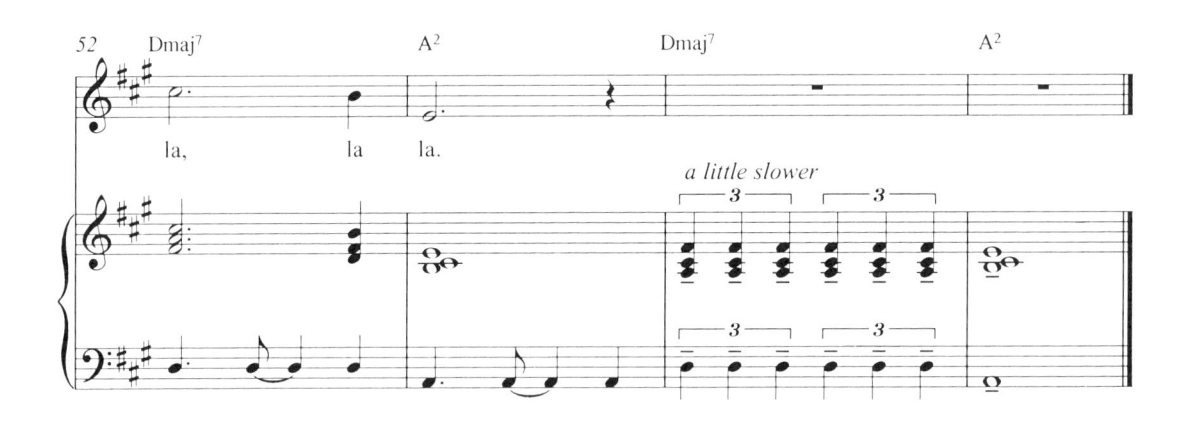

Straight after the song, THOMAS goes up to her.

Thomas *(quite coldly, almost sarcastically)* Mary, if Jesus comes into this room and I can put my finger into the holes in his hands and feet and can put my hand into his side, *then* I'll believe.

Thomas storms off at opposite side. The others just stare at MARY.

Mary Magdalene *(to PETER)* Peter, I suppose *you* don't believe me either.

Peter *(more kindly)* Mary, *(bewildered)* I don't know what to believe.

Mary Magdalene *(cheerfully)* Then I'll go and tell Mary his mother, *she'll* believe me.

Peter *(pointing to the exit on the opposite side)* You'd better go this way. It's safer.

Mary Magdalene *(gently mocking but still cheerful)* Are you *still* afraid, Peter?

MARY MAGDALENE leaves, briskly. PETER turns back to the APOSTLES.

Peter Of course I'm still frightened. They could be coming any moment now.

JESUS appears at the door.

Jesus Don't be afraid. *(all turn towards the door in amazement)* It's me! Peace!

All the APOSTLES rush up to JESUS.

Peter Lord!

James Adonai!

John Messiah!

All *Hosanna!*

All burst into song round JESUS.

14. HOSANNA! (Reprise)

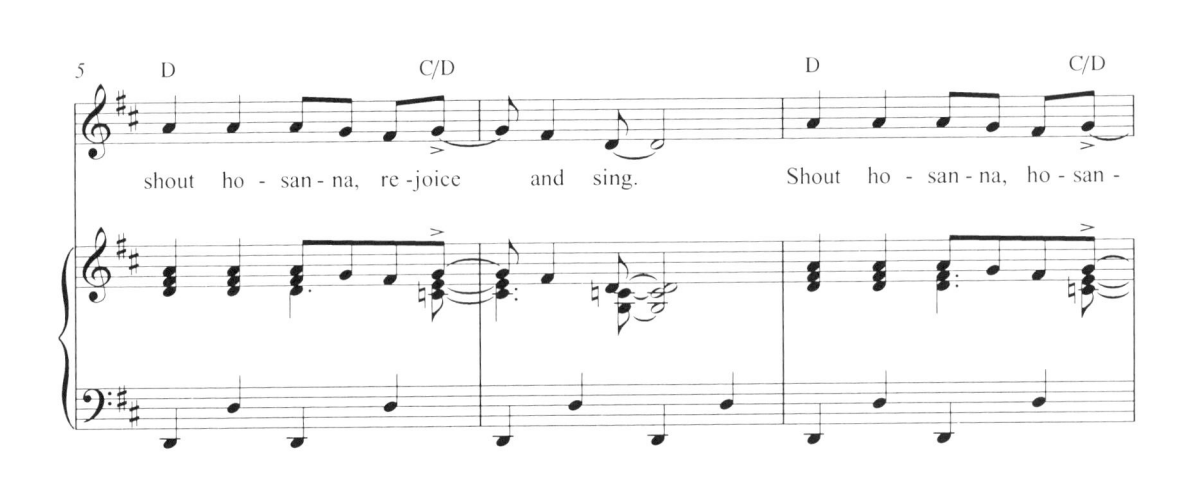

Joyfully ($\quarter = 156$)

Shout hosanna, hosanna, sanna, sanna, shout hosanna, rejoice and sing. Shout hosanna, hosanna, sanna, sanna, shout hosanna to the King of kings.

Shout ho-san-na to the King of kings, Shout ho-san-na!

Shout ho-san-na! Shout ho-san-na to the King of

kings! *(shout)* Ho-san-na!

THOMAS appears at the side again. All turn towards him, but THOMAS hesitates.

Jesus	*(cheerfully and kindly)* Thomas, come here and feel my hands. Come and touch my side.

THOMAS moves slowly towards JESUS, staring in amazement. He does <u>not</u> touch JESUS, but falls down at his feet.

Thomas	*(slowly)* My Lord and my God.

Jesus	Thomas, you believe because you have seen. Blessed are those who have not seen, but still believe. *(to all)* I am now going back to the Father. You must wait here and pray till I send you the Holy Spirit. Then, go out and tell the good news to the whole world.

JESUS disappears from their sight. The APOSTLES remain in silent prayer. The silence is only interrupted by the occasional petitions.

Peter	Come, Holy Spirit, promised by the Lord. Come, fill our hearts and minds.

Silence.

James	Come, Holy Spirit, with your wisdom and strength.

Silence.

Matthew	Come, Holy Spirit, give us your courage and understanding.

Silence.

Andrew	Come, Holy Spirit, with your power!

Silence. The sound of the introduction of the next song is heard. Then the FIRE (children in flowing red costumes) and WIND (children in blue and white costumes) rush in, touching the APOSTLES, singing.

15. WIND AND FIRE / HOSANNA!

With movement - energetically ($\quarternote = 156$)

mf

1: Fire
2: Wind

1. Fire, fire, fire, be touched by the tongues of fire. Fire, fire, fire, tongues of fire.
2. Wind, wind, wind, be swept by the wind of change. Wind, wind, wind, wind of change.

Fire, fire, fire, be touched by the tongues of fire. Fire, fire, fire, tongues of fire.
Wind, wind, wind, be swept by the wind of change. Wind, wind, wind, wind of change.

Burn-ing all your sins a-way, fill-ing you with love to-day;
Now your work has just be-gun, share the news with ev-'ry-one,

28
F/A
Gm/E
Gm
giv - ing you the strength to guide you on your
go and tell the world the won - ders God has
31
A7sus4
A N.C.
Apostles
D
A/C♯
G/B
G/A
D
way. Come on, let's go, go, go, let's go –
done. Come on, let's go, go, go, let's go –
35
A/C♯
G/B
A
D
A/C♯
G/B
A6
A
set the world on fire, go, go, go, set the world on
spread the wind of change, go, go, go, spread the wind of
39
1.
D
A/C♯
G/B
G/A
C
Em7
Asus4
fire.

change, go, go — spread the wind of change, go, go —

spread the wind of change. *(shout)* Ho-

sa-nna! Ho-sa-nna!

Ho-sa-nna!

55
D
C/D
D
C/D
Shout ho - san - na, ho - san - na, san - na, san - na, shout ho - san - na, re - joice
58
D
C/D
and sing. Shout ho - san - na, ho - san - na, san - na, san - na,
61
D
C
D
D
C
shout ho - san - na to the King of kings. Shout ho - san - na to the

64
D
C
D
C
King of kings,
Shout ho - san - na!
Shout ho - san - na!
67
D
C
F/A
C/G
F
C/E
D
Shout ho - san - na
to the King of kings!
ben marcato
70
ff
Ho - san - na!
ff

Please photocopy this page

KEVIN MAYHEW PERFORMANCE LICENCE FORM

We are delighted that you are considering *Hosanna!* for production.
Please note that a performance licence is required and royalties are payable as follows:

10% of gross takings, plus VAT
(Minimum fee: £20.00 + VAT = £23.50)

This form should be returned to the Copyright Department at Kevin Mayhew Ltd. A copy, including our performance licence number, will be returned to you.

Name of Organisation _____

Contact name _____

Contact address _____

_____

Postcode _____ _____

Contact Telephone No. _____ Contact Fax No. _____

E-mail _____

Date(s) of performance(s) _____

Venue _____

Seating capacity _____

Proposed ticket price _____

I undertake to submit performance fees due to Kevin Mayhew Ltd within 28 days of the last performance of *Hosanna!*, together with a statement of gross takings.

Signature _____

Name (please print) _____

On behalf of _____

Address if different from above _____

_____

To be completed by Kevin Mayhew Copyright Department:

Performance Licence No. _____ is issued to _____

for _____ performances of *Hosanna!* on _____

Copyright Department, Kevin Mayhew Ltd, Buxhall, Stowmarket, Suffolk, IP14 3BW
Telephone number: UK 01449 737978   International +44 1449 737978
Fax number: UK 01449 737834   International +44 1449 737834
E-mail: info@kevinmayhewltd.com

Other available titles

Light of the World

by Denis O'Gorman and Barry Hart

1450257
ISBN 1 84003 944 2

Celebrating Jesus

by Denis O'Gorman and Barry Hart

1450253
ISBN 1 84003 911 6

Angels Up High

by Denis O'Gorman and Barry Hart

1450226
ISBN 1 84003 794 6